Demand for new mistakes

Something is wrong if nothing is wrong in your business.

Title rings ever

Normand Rocky
CV Madhavi
C Rajgopal

Most popular mistake

- My employees must adhere to customer mist of business within the box bounds for Customer praise and professional tag and that discomfiture should remember innovative and profit means of business inertia instead of business changes with knowledge and expertise.

Perfect business is dream fulfilled

- Perfect employees are impossible
- Permanent Customer is impossible
- Complete solution in one go is not available
- Competition patronage is a pun
- Regulatory friendship is magic
- Change is always constant in variable market.

Check

- Employees targets if you have no failure or fault
- Competition if you have no fear of losing
- Management ethics if business has no challenge
- Capabilities if technology has no changes
- Profitability if expenditure is not a problem

Good mistakes

- Gain access to others intellect and interest
- Back in hardworking gentleness of shortcuts
- Innovate on skills of avoiding victimization

No complaints

- Leave complacency and complex uncertainty of Customer and other stakeholders
- Let Customer think you are happy playing safe and that discomfiture should switch on the rivals to put off your customers against your business
- Lead learning into disinterested attitude towards Customer.

How come

- A square business is designed without any changes and challenges
- Customer is no dissatisfied ever with your business
- Product is not competed and accepted by buyers
- Check your business credibility.

Business right

- Is not a correct information about good Strategy
- Is corrected anomaly and Customer misconception
- Is detection of business inconsistencies in customer service
- Is not a right of Customer as effort taker but should be your employees' hardwork.

Employees

- Learn from mistakes
- Enjoy failure of experiments
- Risk their skill for Customer praise
- Regard test as rewarding business loyalty

Ode

- Mistakes skate and take Business sense
- Wrong builds trouble with questions
- Aver the error in customer essence
- Fix it and rejoice acceptance
- Welcome interaction without interference

Staff

- Creating inaccuracies should check and change the rules of engagement as needed
- Finds fault but should not blame except for resolution to circumvent delay and chaos
- Should overcome negligence and overdependence.

70% errors come from employees

- Employees commit mistakes
- Under pressure
- When entire team is going astray
- For satisfaction of selfish goals
- To deliberate business devastation
- In ignorant lethargy

Reward vs reword

- Audit and assurance are in the job of finding mistakes or risks go with error exaggerated or excellence eroded in business globally
- Though zero defects are preferred it's a theory compliance not practical in business reality unless mistakes are renamed or reworded, instead of rewarding discovery and corrections.

Limiting the errors

- The goal of avoiding or zilching the errors is unreasonable as much as unattractive in preventing the risk taking advantage of having enough aptitude for corrective learning attitude towards collective learning systems under pressure or other times in the process of conducting business.

Top mistakes

- Need immediate corrections
- Regulatory and compliance requirements if gone awry could close your business success
- Wrong customisation if not managed by right need of Customer can get your resources wasted.

Err to ignore

- You are safe to ignore mistakes with
-   - new business knowledge, numbers and technology because you are not their sources
-   - ads showing pleasant dreams not delivered in product because ads are like fiction
-   - employees but not Customers with Business options in plenty.

Review

- Reveal and revert back to the original ideas if no results are found in no mistake Business
- Business is better off with mistakes and with results
- Mistake is solely Business Strategy gone awry, any other reason is avoidable.

Innocent errors in

- Human reading, interpretation and output
- utilisation gap between old and new resources have to be carefully studied, identified and covered by your complete attention to change.

Innovative mistakes

- Why should the business flow top-down from sales down to profit but not from profit to sales?
- Try to avoid multiple cost burdens in business globally to go for expenditure in ballon payment.
- Interference of science and technology goes wrong for business scared of every employee.

Deadly sins of business

- Override Customer safety concerns
- Know how to get Customer pay
- Work overtime every day
- Fetch sales to get Salary
- Degrade your rival to hide your mistakes.

Wins are

- New mistakes gratified
- Not permanent
- Posts to understanding problem
- Business in unusual turns
- Mistakes corrected
- Tactical gear on practical strategies.

New mistakes

- Advise employees to think of innovative ways that lead to new mistakes with business culture instead of users lost by false hopes but not sure how to cover the difference with correction in the global right stead for results in favour of Business, Customer and economic growth.

Wish-takes

- Customer is wishing to get new products for use in daily improvement in task execution, for your business resources to understand and work with, to again convince users for buying them, more risk means management of mistakes in satisfying customer by service.

Mistakes

- Mean, idiotic, stupid, tricky, arrogant, knack less, ebbs, sickening to prove that the sources are men who are clueless mistakes in walking
- More info states tortuous acceptance of knowledge errors sadly

Rectify others error

- Collective competition in correcting errors of the rivals or picking their errors for new corrections or picking your mistakes for new rival suggestions can get you better market power or learning with quick Customer growth.

Watch easy task

- Mistakes and stake both are high but some important lessons for toughest challenge resolution can be had in easy task
- Employees should be balanced and overcome artificial success of doing easy task by digging innovative ways from it.

Capacity dynamics

- Even machines are in need of Customer scale and employees' involvement with risk of getting ruined by experiment, paradoxical but demands balance of bolts and jolts, holds and joints
- The changes can get a new role of machine for next lifestyle progression.

Speed of Customer

- Can think of innovative solutions from your business to different companies that go into future challenges or opportunities or garbage can depending upon the market path or user perspective and business developments continuously tested on skills and information.

Business fate

- Fortune favours the customer
- Team with employee who is brave and ethical but not winner
- Save same ethics for business as customer
- Motivated employees should motivate Customers, not sell to them.

Repeating correct methods

- Business is in repeating correct methods instead of mistakes that are correct unless discovered
- Repeat corrections instead of mistakes
- Do not hesitate to ask for redirection in doubtfulsituations to avoid repetition of mistakes.

Twist mistake

- Instead of losing Customer over twisted facts it's better to challenge mistake so that we can gain confidence by twisting mistake that is re-visiting, reportraying or repairing the damage to your immediate stakeholder benefit.

User value

- Each customer should get unique business treatment based on the market, need and values.
- Every user invests money, time and consideration for economic inclusion of multiple projects on Companies selling various different products to customers.

Knowledge allocation

- Modern business is more of traditional values and less into devotion for obsolescence in machine for knowledge to be lead player in customer satisfaction coming from right solution provided by technologies trying to remind and revive the best of Customer and business developments, so use knowledge wisely, neither excess nor deficit in a business effect.

Check your business success

- Are all your employees coming and leaving in time or following different times but not everyone adhering to policy?
- Are you not having enough Customer complaints but some extra sales?
- As you are competing, are your rivals against you or collaborative with other companies?

Drain your business

- Enlarge the process and scope for mistakes because anyway no failure leads to no success
- Change to the latest knowledge, spend high on technology, challenge employees to break out of the box of work ethics
- Give customers price for products unimaginable of rivalry tactics.

Train users

- It will keep your employees up-to-date with customers and product features or your new employee hires will be newer than Customers and have to learn from Customer in business naiveities.

Better the scope of strategic errors

- Try more and often for another error in the same process for the large level solutions in better deals on future Strategic risk mitigation and adaptation of business with globalisation change racing to meet new demands of Customer in different options unravelled in the same problem or mistakes.

Including guards and checks

- Train employees to understand the need for giving more accurate change suggestions that should be preventing errors from beginning but some extra knowledge and patience for rectification of mistakes should be cultivated in business stakeholders. The care must be able to get out of mistake committing scenarios.

Organise skills

- Knowledge has to be updated to reflect the views of best change within physical value balancing quality or consumption tastes of acquiring skills and retaining the required interest of customer in adjusting with new ways to future business ventures evolving around changes in the extent of 90% to get affected by new skill and tool combination.

Invite reason

- Investment imbalance due to diversification needs, lack of skill or other business changes are not allowed to get the best return for more risk because of your customers to follow market for new products that help better than your business products.

Deal with the best

- Business is designed with avoiding the unavoidable-mistake, reason, failure, waste, risk
- Get help and business representatives to best technologies, product, management, market, Innovation and entrepreneurship but some extra patience for unavoidable circumstances in the business administration.

Optimising of machines

- Use the best methods for optimum resource strategies, planning and development project that will help customers certainly not the market way to utilise technology that goes along new form of mutual growth of your customers to make it complete value chain gain by providing specific product utilisation.

Contextual errors

- Value
- Don't forget your past failure to be strong and free in the process of misplacing Customer understanding with your business stakeholders
- The context of employees is customer.

User should err

- The company should show how much you are happy with the global community mistakes without any conditions.
- The learning and business changes increase in quality of Customer as trying hard to get multiple facets out on mistakes though.

Capture innovation in action

- The company should show how to get innovation working in the market beforehand of taking Customer feedback or rival suggestions for new global effect of community Innovation

Utility is not full

- The product should be free from any mistakes with the given usage and experience should give out more ways of fixing new errors in business reaching greater utility within full exploitation of business products.

Risk factors

- Product passes through quality control tests without any defects
- Employees performance management shows no gaps
- Competition analysis reveals no threat
- Market throws no challenges.

Figure out more challenges

- Increasing quality of solutions and business developments up with guaranteed restoration of business environment and external market values could not be possible without waiting for Customer challenge with impossible demands.

Plan your next error

- The changes that are unpredictability drivers cannot support but some business planning and preparation of handling could help with your future mistakes in market strategy by controlling the process deviations and business discrepancies in interpretation of market signals.

Business equilibrium

- Study market for marring competitors and their disadvantages from snatching your customers
- Deriving your business equilibrium of giving what Customers want, is better than quitting after following the rival response.

Reverse errors

- The company should work backward to understand what all went wrong in different levels of business implementation to get the complete corrections instead of one.

Pontificating errors

- The market laughs at business foolishness
- The competition rips through others' errors
- The company tries to avoid errors
- The employees blame other stakeholders
- The customer forgets the errors in the corrections.

User errors

- The company knows itself behind making every product for users who are buying them for different reasons and expectations or criteria because of what errors in usage, performance, perception and feedback leading to product failure for future.

Deck of Customer input

- Mistakes in the business side are not intended outputs to improve upon the market path of utilisation of capabilities and information to get new impact for your business customers but each customer complaint should be treated as input on Innovation.

Current position

- Technology is medium, technique is its method, employee is that operator who turns out more useful products from process attribution in which mistake or defect can occur in any state of products from inception to completion of the allocated use for specific period or need.

Technology should

- Be exploited in maximum relevance of competitive advantage to get multiple ideas flow steady under any conditions of Customer as your buyer or market as your judge.

Explore competitors

- To connect with their knowledge that is the need for your response
- To understand their mistakes in removing repetition from your side
- To get new impact of their capabilities on your decisions

Operational improvement

- Success leads to learning with market action in future irrespective of the operation defects and improvements can get better customer insight into how to use machine for next leadership advantages of Innovation.

Hi-tech àgility

- Is this Technological flexibility to get new pace around momentum of responding in the competitive styles backed by solid Strategic response, latest technologies and business changes.

Use technology in

- Professional adherence to Customer needs before rivals give better response
- Product innovation and excellence by running a great operations drive
- Preparation for fulfillment by associating precision tactics and not some automation in user interest

Customer experience

- Product comes with experience that goes along services in your bit with response following user feedback to get the ease of flowing through Customer demands or requests for your skill at the product that is new idea converted into different experience.

Tackle common need

- The competition and consumer can benefit from the market path of feeding community value in addition to serving the common need of Customer as your culture of trust built on the market offering

Current inclusions

- Technology is related to experience patterns altering organisation dynamics and Customer preferences by allowing market imperfections to get new impact of Innovation.

Getting started

- With a new window in business etiquette rather than product innovation can get better overall value of quality or performance of products and solutions that are sought by Customer who wants to be in open Strategy Innovation.

Check your business

- Success stories could wait for market assessment but not Business weaknesses that must be fixed urgently
- Product is at risk of getting outdated
- Credibility by Customer commitment is better than your business products

Total technology

- Innovation is no longer having good affiliation with Technology inclusion but considering Customer views can grow total innovation focus of future modern solutions in controlled Technology environment.

Grasping the market

- Knowledge concepts and Customer satisfaction should not deviate from the market path of business changes brought by external challenges and experiments with your business rivalry.

Use mistakes

- To connect with different companies at assessment of different business models in motivation of company operational excellence for Customer involvement with learning and thinking changes.

Bring true value

- Worth of global value chain can't be predicted but some extra Innovation in accepting through pangs of business changes brought by Customer demands can get you better market credibility or market trust by Customer participation in business transformation.

Change mistakes

- Best efficiency and business results could affect your business mistakes at different levels of operations development for your skill of changing them in favour of user or investor, say on grounds of business ethics

Business capabilities

- Come from capacities of business resources reducing the risk and issues including cost of operations at obtaining your outputs in customer direction offering company capability in support of Customer need.

Benefits of technology

- Skills are used in precision of the product performance
- Value perfection in business globally to follow Customers changes utility of technology that could compare better than employee.

Verify mistakes

- Are there any mistakes really or are you doing smart business with steps that are identifying the smallest deviation of avoiding penalties of mistakes with rivals, Customer and internal environment?

Best efforts

- Best outcome is not in conclusion but as increasing journey attaching importance or enjoyments in getting customer satisfactory effort and business involvement with the intended balance on one another's goal.

Ab or ebb

- Absolutes to be taken as trusted by more business collaboration towards Customer
- Ebb tide of business decline comes when buyers on different occasions compare better than your product that calls for new business attempt as new opportunity.

Mistakes count

- As proof of preparation for avoiding penalties
- Towards building your own market power by allowing interference of technology and business representatives before Customer.

Objectives and goals

- The changes in the direction of economy by high industry growth-oriented Customer development through a good corporate management and responsibility is your single goal.

By industry

- User segment does know how much you can win adjusting to industry standard in the quality of Customer expectations by customised endorsement or Innovative competition in reducing the risk of market transitions.

Business Euphemism

- I will continue to invest in employees
- Customer is a VIP, or value Innovation purchaser
- Strategic base of business changes with technology.

Pool networks

- To connect in business globally from knowledge of customers as a new collation for combining resources and information of different customer segments in understanding Customer community to work for self formed groups.

Cool Innovation

- The changes can get a better business innovation in the process of establishing interaction based improvement when Customer needs superiority for ability to ensure intelligent communication on Innovation required.

Cultural value

- Bring happiness of Customer in future changes with technology or process culture improvement on alignment of business and user culture with value balancing growth by culture upliftment brought for new products.

Bugs

- Are mistakes in irritation of Customer as even they could allow critical deviations to be pretext for promoting business innovation of competition in offering worth and complications at the same time.

Managing mistakes

- Customers can blame anything or anybody from the business and stakeholders can shift it from one another but not on Customer, employees are not stopped from blaming machine or others in the company while interacting with community for correction of mistakes in their side.

Recorrect Technology

- Using the same Technology at different levels of task improvement or approach alignment in the business interests of promoting products in adapting to customer aspirations can help reinventing the Technology for new business fit with market.

Change is

- Like the check on possible Business block in skills, forecast, Customer understanding, technology relevance, research management or operational Innovation in the direction of getting sureshot persistent business leadership.

Dereliction of Customer

- Duty mistakes are inevitable but employees get new trouble with negligence of Customer so that can not be ignored or forgiven for affecting the personal self as compared to every single problem affecting policy and business changes.

Naming mistake

- Don't remember mistake by seeing employees or vice versa because then attrition can grow worse and lessons can be dying as values of person leaving the organisation
- Don't also know mistakes by Customer who wants one output and nothing else.

Mistakes in

- Mood iteration see task aversive knowledge emitting swings
- More intricate sound test automation keenness evaluate system
- Mean idiotic stupid tactics avoiding knowledge exchange simply.

Type1

- Mistakes are committed but not known
- Customers may turn out to be in the receiving end of such high defect output, business may lose credibility or capabilities as rivals turn out better products.

Type2

- Mistakes are anticipated but not committed though employees think of even corrections that are later useful opportunity creators but not always getting a difference of growth and Customer satisfaction.

M3

- M3 mistakes are made and known for saving time with correction though they could create change or added wastage in occurences for your business credibility to be restored.

M4

- Mistakes are not commited and not known
- Competitive analysis or their lessons can help with your business success without guilt of losing capabilities over mistakes.

Missing on mistakes

- No problem might see you opening door to new opportunities or problems or exaggerated delays in business implementation because no mistakes occur when you do not work for anything.

Marketing mistakes

- No business representation but only happy exaggeration to waste budget without stopping by other department dependency
- Ignorance of competitive similarity of business products or senseless challenge with rivals
- Lack of effort precision on Customer end.

Financial mistakes

- Wrong customisation cost-benefit analysis that goes without giving variance corrections
- Misallocation of the business and market resources against changes with investment losses pooling financial mistakes never turning on audits but leading to bankruptcy.

Operational mistakes

- Lack of understanding of Customer hassle gets more inefficiencies in business administration to begin with and poor experience in user end later slowing your business success to throw unseen future mistakes in market chain of losing brand leader image.

Business means

- Bugs, unwarranted system idiosyncrasies, new error signalling sugar-coated effect on winning Customer under process of constant corrections of inevitable mistakes in more reducing cost of redundant inevitability.

Company should

- Muster technology to master the various mistakes in probable occurence whether explicitly by your actions or competition or market participants or community because this is how recession in economy knows its entry.

Mistakes should try

- To connect in different processes, cultures and means of reaching greater perfection in the understanding of business to-dos on Customer motivation.

Thank you

- Please make notes and let me know your business mistakes at pondolint@gmail.com

www.ingramcontent.com/pod-product-compliance
Lightning Source LLC
Chambersburg PA
CBHW020555220526
45463CB00006B/2309